RÛNARMÂL I

RÛNARMÂL I

The RÛNA-Talks
Summer 1991ev

Stephen Edred Flowers

Copyright © 2017
Lodestar

All rights reserved. No part of this book, either in part or in whole, may be reproduced, transmitted or utilized in any form or by any means electronic, photographic or mechanical, including photocopying, recording, or by any information storage and retrieval system, without the permission in writing from the Publisher, except for brief quotations embodied in literary articles and reviews.

For permissions, or for the serialization, condensation, or for adaptation write the Publisher at the address below.

Published by
Lodestar
P.O. Box 16
Bastrop, Texas 78602

runa@texas.net

Abbreviations

Gk.   Greek
Heb. Hebrew
OE   Old English
ON   Old Norse
tr.   translator

Stylistic Notes

The use of capital letter needs to be explained: When a word is spelled with a capital letter in violation of normal rules of capitalization in current American English usage, it is an indication that the word is being used in its archetypal, ideal or absolute sense. In speaking this is done with a voice inflection, it writing with a capital letter.

Words set in all-capitals are being labeled as key-words which both encapsulate and describe entire Worlds.

Acknowledgments

Thanks go to Anthea for her reading and editing of the original typescript, and to Timothy »Drachenherz« Weinmeister for the cover graphic.

Contents

General Introduction
1

RÛNA-Talk OOO
On the Thews
5

RÛNA-Talk OO
The Power of the Word in Operant Runology
9

RÛNA-Talk I
The Words and the Word: Auxiliary Formulæ
19

RÛNA-Talk II
The Polarian Method and RÛNA
23

RÛNA-Talk III
Universalizing the System
27

RÛNA-Talk IV
Head Staves
31

RÛNA-Talk O
Transformation and RÛNA
35

RÛNA-Talk V
Is RÛNA for All?
37

RÛNA-Talk VI
RÛNA and WYRD
41

RÛNA-Talk VII
Modeling and Re-Modeling of Self and Culture
45

RÛNA-Talk VIII
RÛNA as a Trans-Æonic Word
49

Glossary
55
Bibliography
59

General Introduction

The RÛNA-Talks
Summer of 1991ev

In the Summer of 1991ev I delivered a series of eight RÛNA-Talks at the now-infamous Manor-House, located at 5908 Manor Road in Austin, Texas. In the beginning, I told only James Chisholm of my intention to give these talks, which would be open to any one who wished to listen, and hear. They would be designed for no particular "school of thought." the talks would be attended by individuals of all kinds of backgrounds and levels of understanding. I would give them at 11:00 am, every Saturday morning— not a time calculated to be particularly convenient for people to attend. But that was my intention. I was determined to give the talks, regardless of whether any one was there to hear them or not. They would in fact constitute magical utterances to the objective universe, if there were people there fine, if not, the utterances would have their effects anyway.

On the occasion of the first talk, I indeed began speaking to an empty room. I had been talking for about 15 minutes when Mr. Chisholm came to the front of the house to hear the talk. Eventually there would be as many as 15 people at the talks. But word of the presentations spread Runically— with no overt effort on my part.

The talks themselves were delivered from sparse noted outlines consisting of only a few words. What follows are papers generated from those notes at a later date, they are not transcripts of what was said nor are they verbatim reports. In fact they have only now been put into concrete form. Their contents therefore inevitably reflect in some small ways developments of RÛNA between 1991 and 1995. The Talks had their purpose, these written documents a somewhat different one.

The eight RÛNA-Talks are prefaced with a presentation of a talk delivered to the Rune-Gild in February of 1991ev, this is designated RÛNA-Talk OOO, and by another talk I gave at the New York Open Center on the evening of May 31, 1991, just prior to beginning the RÛNA-Talks at the Manor-House. A version of this Open Center talk was also given in March of 1991 at the Manor-House. I designate this RÛNA-Talk OO. There was also a talk delivered to a select audience on July 18, and which fell outside the Saturday cycle. This is designated as RÛNA-Talk O, and is placed in its chronological position in the sequence of talks.

The title of the present volume, *RÛNARMÂL*, is an Icelandic word which literally means the "Speech of Mystery," or the "Sayings of the Rune." In these talks the Rune, or the Mystery is allowed to speak. In the course of the talks, the reader/listener will learn of the character of the Word RÛNA and how it came to me to be Spoken.

RÛNA is a Word in the magical or initiatory sense. It is, in the terminology of the Rune-Gild, a Working Word of an Erulian, or in the more universalistic terminology of the Temple of Set, the Word of a Magus. Such Words encapsulate and encode an entire philosophy, and from the Word the entire philosophy can be derived— at least by its Speaker. It then becomes the Work and the Woe of the Speaker to articulate this philosophy to the World at large. Such Words by their very character create and destroy worlds, whole worlds undergo reconfigurations in accordance with the meaning and shape of the Word.

To Hear such a Word is humbling, because the enormity of what lies outside one's Self is made clear and present. This causes great Woe. But to have to Speak such a Word forth is yet more humbling. In this one comes face to face with the enormity of the Work which lies ahead. To Hear and have to Speak such a Word is not the normal course of initiatory development in connection with the Runes or anything else. This process makes utter failure possible in the initiatory life of the individual. Life and sanity can be shattered. Without Hearing and Speaking such a Word an individual may make progress in the initiatory process into infinity. But for change to occur in the World as a whole, or even throughout large portions of the objective universe in general, such Words must be Heard and Spoken forth by certain individuals at certain times in order to further the eternal cycles of Wyrd.

Please read each of the talks on its own terms. This collection represents pieces of a greater puzzle. It is my Work and Woe to present the pieces, to provide the guidelines, but it is essential, if I am to be successful in articulating the Runes that *you* put the pieces together yourself and discover for yourself the essence of the mystery before you. Understanding of the Rune(s) is based on a combination of Knowledge and Work, which raises one's Being— and from that raised horizontal vision Understanding is derived. Such knowledge can not be inserted into a person's brain as if the task at hand were something akin to a freshman English composition paper with the process assignment: "How to Fix a Flat Tire." The inFormation contained here will open doors in an infinite constellation of ways. All who Hear something in them will open to the Rune in their own unique ways.

The talks, and this volume in general, are intended to expand the field of activity of those who deal with the Runes beyond what has become the "conventional" arena of Runic activity. The RÛNA describes a philosophy which, although perhaps ideally suited to the Germanic tradition, is present in all legitimate traditions and in the deep-level experience of most humans. The aim of the *RÛNARMÂL* is to begin to make the essence of RÛNA accessible to all who would Hear the Word, regardless of the School of Initiation to which they belong.

I would like to thank all of those who attended the talks in 1991 and who therefore gave their contents the opportunity to be Heard in the World: Crystal Dawn, James A. Chisholm, Dianne Ross, John Gyori, Dee Pye, Don Webb, Rosemary Webb, Michael Rigby, Adriane Carrico, Guðni Elisson, Edward van Cura— and many others whose names remain unknown.

Stephen EDRED Flowers
14 February 1996ev/XXXI
Woodharrow

Reyn til Rúna!

RÛNA-Talk OOO

On the Thews

There are four kinds of thews, or virtues, to be recognized. Some are to be practiced by all, some by only the few.

I
Doing Right among Men

The first sort of thew (virtue) consists of doing Right among Men: These are the so-called *civil virtues*. To fulfill this virtue one is to perform actions according to Tradition. Virtue always has an *aim* or *goal*. In the Troth this is embodied in the Nine Noble Virtues (thews). The aims of these virtues are embodied in one of, or any group of, Six Goals: Right (justice), Wisdom (self-development), Might (Power), Harvest (Wealth), Frith (Security and Peace) and Love (Pleasure). Also, in a Troth context one is obligated to give honor to the Gods and Goddesses of one's ancestors.

To fulfill this thew (virtue), one is to perform actions according to tradition. Performance entails visible actions. Correct performance brings the praise of the most noble of one's fellows.

II
Recognition of the Separateness
of an Individual's Soul-Life

The second kind of thew consists of being able to recognize the Soul-Life of the individual as being separate from the Body-Life. Disciplines which teach this virtue have been called by some "cleansing" or "purifying" ones. We might wish to call them "strengthening" virtues. Their performance brings a Knowledge and Experience of the gap between Soul and Lyke (body). The action exercised in this virtue is entirely internal and its result is a hallowing, or "sanctification" of the Self. Only the few will wish to cross the barrier which separates the performance of the first kind of thew and the second. The effort to do so is extraordinary— beyond the ordinary.

III
Intellectual Thews

Intellectual thews bring Knowledge and Understanding of the contents of the Soul or Mynd. Here the contents of the Soul are explored and Re-Called from the deep Well of Remembrance (Mímir's Well). Performance entails separating the contents of the Soul from the Body-Life, and realizing them in a conscious way. Correct performance grants a sanctified (*wîh-*)state, wherein the Runes, the Mysteries, can be unlocked. This internal work, of the Self, is contained (for the most part) in *The Nine Doors of Midgard*.

IV
Working Rightly
in the World

The fourth kind of thew Works with (by means of) the *bond* between Self and the Right Forms of Action. These could be called the Paradigms of Righteousness. *Engaged* in this process of Knowledge— having gained a kind of union with the eternal essence within — the subject (the doer of the actions) proceeds to Work Rightly in the *worlds*. Chief among these are the works of restoring *health* and *wholeness* to the world of Midgard. This is done by infusing consciousness and knowledge into the material world. What has been Learned must also be Taught— passed on to one's fellows. This completes the cycle.

*   *
*   *

The four thews describe a process. Each thew is also in and of itself a process. Process I requires belief in, and loyalty to, the traditional principles of one's folk and fellows, while Processes II-IV are internal and transformative ones. The latter three are only Necessary for true Odians. In these thews one trains one's self to realize the separate natures of body and soul/mynd. Having done this one explores, and unlocks in a disciplined way, the Runes (secrets) held in the soul. Once those are known — and have become the *objects* of one's knowledge — one unites one's self with these Runes and thus *become* their powers. The first actions of such a transformed soul will be enactments, in practical ways, of the divine powers attained. The world will be renewed and healed in physical reality.

The following diagram depicts the relationships of the four processes to each other:

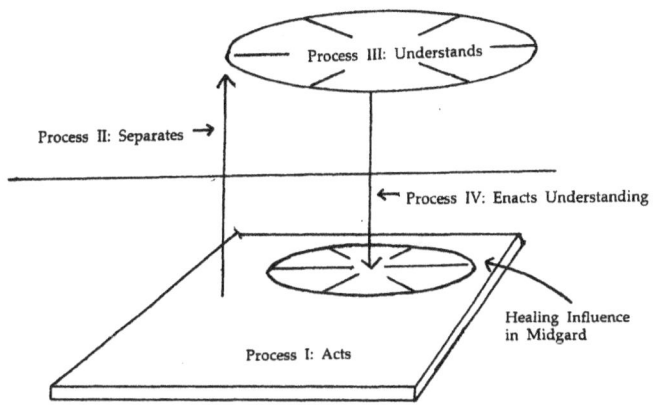

The whole of the four-fold process described is one of creating a link, or bond, of action with the goals of the Gods— that is with the *ginnregin* ("divine advisors"). These are the entities which inForm our souls in a divine— eternal and more perfect way. The bond is sealed by Deeds and not by Thoughts alone.

It is little known that at one time Midgard was more noble than Asgard— it was more *perfect* (completed). But because Midgard is less well shielded from the thurs-forces it has fallen more rapidly into a state of decay. This state can only be repaired through the creation of conduits for the patterns of the *ginnregin* to manifest themselves in Midgard.

What has gone before is a description of how this can be done: with the path of the four ways of virtuous action.

RÛNA-Talk 00

The Power of the Word in Operant Runology

Here I take a rare opportunity to be able to realize an ambitious goal of taking up two difficult tasks: the first is to explain the meaning and function of the Word "Rune" in the Germanic tradition, and the second is to explain how this Word is the source of a fully expressed system of operative symbology, or semiotics.

I will use the somewhat idiosyncratic form of the word "rune": RÛNA throughout when referring to the special sense of *the* Rune, *the* Mystery.

The concept of the Word is of tremendous importance to the Germanic tradition— as is the Work (or Deed) which is directly linked to it. The Word is the intelligible, symbolic, supersensible Form or Principle upon which true and real Work, or Deeds, or actions of any real kind, is based.

This complex is made most explicit, in as few words as possible in the Eddic poem "Hávamál" (stanza 141) when after Óðinn has "taken up" the Runes, the Mysteries of the Universe, he utters:

Orð mér af orði   orðz leitaði
verk mér af verki   verks leitaði

One word, from a word   led me to another word
One work, from a work   led me to another work.*

As is to be expected from the *Edda*, a great deal of wisdom is condensed into a few words. The *experience* which is being described, on a grand scale, is that which happens when a

---

* These lines of Old Norse poetry, though their meaning is clear in the original, virtually defy translation into modern English. The verb *leita,* 'to seek,' takes the genitive case, hence the forms *orðz* and *verks* are the objects what is "sought."

whole great set of complex ideas, and entire philosophy of life and the universe has been transmitted into a mind — by means of direct inspiration. At that point chain reactions of meaning are set off which know no limits. The mind explodes in a hail of meaningfulness. One Word leads to more words, to an infinity of words— that is to say to an infinity of ideas and principles given form and intelligibility through sounds and shapes. These do not, however, remain in the abstract— but are of Necessity (of Need) translated at once into Action— into Deeds. Real ideas can not be contained in the mind alone, but must be expressed in the world of doing.

The original *Word*, that is, the original *idea*, or *thought*, is RÛNA: "the Sense of the Hidden or Unknown." In that one Word all the Mysteries (Runes) are contained. From this one Word (Principle) all the Runes are derived from within the matrix of the Mind (= *hugr/minni/óðr*). At once the Divine Mind (i.e. Óðinn as the archetype of the Mind) begins to articulate the essential and unknowable Mystery into "Words." In traditional Germanic lore these are the *names* of the twenty-four (or sixteen) Runestaves. The one whole Mystery (Rune) has been analyzed into component parts, which even when added together do not quite equal the whole.

This aspect of the tradition embodied in the essence of RÛNA is, for example, that which certain misinformed rune-mystics and diviners in the middle of the 20th century have apparently tried to ascribe to the "blank rune." This is an inauthentic and extremely counter-productive concept because it gives shape and *physical* form (and hence limitation) to something that is in fact without limit and definite form.

These ideas are tantamount to actions because they as a matter of course lead directly to actions and deeds— Works. Without them Works are impossible, because without them they would have no meaning, shape or willed intent. Works are (re-)shapings of reality and the "stuff" of the cosmos.

Under the direction of these Words, Óðinn undertook the re-shaping of the universe by sacrificing his ultimate progenitor, Ymir, and with the material of his "body" the cosmos was reconfigured in a rational mode.

The Hidden gives birth to Words and from Words Deeds are carried out and transformations of all sorts are effected.

Certain Words (seed-words) contain entire complex philosophies and cosmologies latent and most usually unconscious in their forms. These entire philosophies are encoded in a single *Word*. The relationship between the external form of the Word and the hidden philosophy encoded in it is what is meant by a "Rune." The idea that a Word-formula can at once conceal and reveal something. From such a Word the whole complex, articulated (now conscious) philosophy can be derived.

Such Words are like seeds. In the acorn is contained the entire oak, *in potentia*. From the acorn the whole of the oak can be unfolded through time— given the right conditions at the right times.

The ultimate Secret, the highest of all the Runes, is in fact contained in the concept of the very Word RÛNE itself— in the concept of the Unknown, which, when grasped makes the fullness of the Gifts of the Gods manifest in ourSelves.

In the Eddic poem called the "Vafþruðnismál" a hidden reference is made to this concept. This poem is in the form of a riddling context between an unknown stranger and an extremely knowledgeable etin (giant) named Vafþruðnir. Etins are so knowledgeable because they have lived so long. Their "genetic material" is far more primitive and deeply rooted in time than is that of Gods or Men. The Stranger and the Etin bet each other their heads on who is more wise. The contest goes on for a very long time with no conclusion. The etin pushes the Stranger to the limit— so far in fact that the Stranger has to pull his "ace-card" when, in stanza 50, he asks:

hvat mælti Óðinn,   áðr á bál stigi,
    sjálfr í eyra syni?

What did Óðinn whisper   in the ear of his son,
when Baldr was laid   on the funeral pyre?

As this question is posed, the etin realizes that the Stranger is indeed Óðinn himSelf— for the answer to the question is the highest and most unKnowable of the Mysteries. Hence it is the one the etin can not answer, and so looses his head. The essence of this secret transcends the ability of the etin-mind to comprehend in any event. Only Æsir and Men can fully Understand the meaning of this Rune.

The great German philologist, Franz Rolf Schröder, even concluded that the Word whispered in Baldr's ear was the Word RÛNE itself.

My experience leads me to the same conclusion. Such a Whispering by a God, by *the* God of the Mind, whispered into a dead ear brings life eternal and resonates throughout the Ages of Gods and Men.

I know, because I Heard the Word being whispered into my ear in the summer of 1974.

It has been my experience that when a real God speaks to you a single Word will suffice for a lifetime. So great is the power of divine speech.

How I Heard the Word

At one point I was a hopeless occultnik. One with potential, perhaps. But that could be said of most occultniks at some early point in their careers. I became familiar with all the "secrets" to be found in the "occult book shops" of Austin, Texas in 1973 and 1974.

During this time I went to a "psychic fair" in Dallas where a Tibetan monk of European descent did stage-magic to the amazement of the audience. It all seemed like miracles.

In late June of that year, a wiccan "high priestess" of my acquaintance, who happened to be leading the coven my then-girlfriend was a member of, claimed to be in telepathic communication with this Tibetan monk. They were linked in their dreams, it seemed. We should go and meet this monk, and learn his secrets, the high priestess suggested. So off I went, for the ride and for the adventure it might bring. Certainly the monk will welcome us with open arms— he knows the high priestess in his dreams.

It seemed he lived outside Houston, Texas. No doubt in some remote location. We arrived at his unlikely Shambhala— in the middle of an oil-field. His front yard was scattered with the debris of several of those "do-it-yourself" sports car kits— probably left over from the 1960s. The high priestess braved the front door. We waited in the car. The monk emerged, robed in a T-shirt (a bit too small for his Buddha-like belly)— and carrying a can of his favorite adult beverage. (The kind that bull terrier used to hawk, I believe.) The conversation at the door was short. The high priestess returned to the car. (His wisdom must be pure to have taken such a short time to convey.) "He's not ready to meet me," the high priestess mumbles, trying to put the best face on an embarrassing situation.

The drive home to Austin was a silent one. I sat in the back seat, dozing. Then, audibly, in my ear I Heard the a sound [roonah], which is the Word, RÛNA. At once I knew what the word referred to: the Germanic writing system of pre-Christian times. I'd seen reference to them in Jacob Grimm and elsewhere. At once I felt what it was I should do.

We arrived back in Austin on Sunday night. Monday I skipped my linguistics class and went to the main library of the University of Texas at Austin. The library was at that time housed in the Tower. I checked a wide variety of books on the subject of "runes." Among them Wolfgang Krause's first edition of the older runic inscriptions entitled *Runeninschriften im älteren Futhark* (1937) and his short handbook *Was man in Runen ritzte* (1935), but Karl Spiesberger's *Runenmagie* (1955) also found its way into my stack of titles. This volatile mixture of books, most of which had not been opened or read for years, was the first milestone in my journey. The way was opened when the Word signifying the ultimate Mystery was whispered in my ear, as it resonated over the eternal cycle of Ages.

Again it was time to go forth from the Gates of Valhalla. The Eternal Work — *das ewige Werk* — was to be renewed and reawakened.

The point of this story is that even on the most absurd of journey, if it is undertaken in the spirit of seeking the mysteries, reward can be found. The seeking must take place, both inwardly and outwardly. Physical journeys are essential to real exploration— yet no mystery will be revealed merely by making pilgrimage to place x, y, or z.

The story of Columbus' "discovery" of America is a case in point. He went out looking for one thing: a direct sea-route to India, and found another: a whole "new world." The fact is that the man died not even knowing (or admitting to himself what the truth was) that he had stumbled upon something which would alter his world. Modern-day seekers for mysteries often find themselves in similar situations. One thing is sought, but another, perhaps greater thing is found— if the seeker remains open to the unexpected and does not allow preconceptions to cloud the experience of discovery.

The Germanic myth of Óðinn as the seeker the Unknown who is willing to sacrifice anything, including his own Self, to attain it is the most complete archetype for the seeker in the realm of divine mythologies. He sought for the Unknown (RÛNA), found it in a flash and was able to remain psychically intact in order to analyze, explore, and articulate the essence of the Unknown in the form of what we have historically received as the Runic Tradition. This same archetype continued to resonate in the Germanic soul right into modern times. The myth of Faust, willing to "sell his soul to the Devil," that is, willing to give himself to himself, in order to gain knowledge, power and pleasure— is but a further extension of the Odinic archetype.

I Heard the Word in what appears to be an unlikely time and place. But a whole constellation of factors came into play, across the multi-dimensional vistas of WYRD, in order to make what was Heard intelligible, and what was intelligible workable.

The Concept: RÛNA

RÛNA means *the* Secret or Mystery (Rune), and the ultimate Secret is housed in the concept of Secrecy itself. It is not that something is being consciously concealed, it is a matter of approaching the Form or Principle of Hiddenness itself which lies at the root of the mystery.

RÛNA is a noun, but its force, its effect, if you will, is dynamic and verbal.

The novelist John Fowles, writing in his philosophical treatise *The Aristos* (p. 28), explains this phenomenon quite well when he says:

> Mystery, or unknowing, is energy. As soon as a mystery is explained, it ceases to be a source of energy. If we question deep enough there comes a point where answers, if answers could be given, would kill. We may want to dam the river; but we dam the spring at our peril. In fact, since 'God' is unknowable, we cannot dam the spring of basic existential mystery. 'God' is the energy of all questions and questing; and so the ultimate source of all action and volition.

Continuing with Fowles' metaphor for a moment, the Rune (RÛNA) is the ultimate source of all waters, and the runestaves are the springs feeding the rivers of meaning in this world of Midgard.

Also when confronting the very concept of the Secret itself we soon come up against an ancient dichotomy: a polarization of ideas. Such polarizations are not an obstacle, but a bridge for the Runer. There are the "Secrets of Nature," and the "Secrets of the Soul." This describes the two poles of RÛNA—one *outer* ("out there," in Nature) and one *inner* ("in here," in the mind, soul or spirit of the individual human being.)

Scientists spend their time trying to "figure out" the "secrets of nature." The fact that there is, much to most' scientist's chagrin, a great deal of the Mystery in what they are trying to do is revealed by the curious, but well-known and uncontested phenomenon that occurs whenever one of these scientists unravels a "secret of nature." The first thing that happens is that a myriad of "new secrets" present themselves to be unraveled. The scientist is not creating the Known, but the Unknown.

At the same time mystics spend their time trying to "figure out" the "secrets of the psyche." Many, especially in our modern age, attempt to do so by looking to scientific methods, and by seeking to "demystify" magic.

Both the "scientist" and the "mystic" most usually miss the point of their endeavors because they consider themselves on the *same* path (in the case of the "modern mystic" who says things such as "magic is just undiscovered science," or they see themselves as absolutely unrelated to one another (as is most often the case with the materialistic technician).

In reality these tendencies betray the fact that these are two polar opposites, with both existing on the same spectrum. This is why each contains the seed of its opposite in practice. The Runer, one aware of, and working with, RÛNA, is conscious of this polarity and is able through this knowledge to avoid the pitfalls inherent in the situations.

Manifestations of these two Runes (inner and outer) are present in the symbolism of each of the runestaves. The basic definition of RÛNA as "Sense of the Hidden" accounts for both ends of this spectrum. The *sense* is an inner, subjective, noumenon, while the *hidden* itself is an outer, objective, phenomenon.

So the question looms: *What are we to do with this knowledge*? The answer to that question is contained in the galdor: *reyn til runa*! This is an Icelandic phrase which means alternately: "seek the mysteries," or "try for the mysteries."

Galdor
Verbal-Magic

Galdor is the true word for "rune-magic," or operant runology. It might also be called "verbal magic," or "word magic" (*magia verbis*).

The root of understanding how operant runology works is the realization that a Runestave is principally made up of three components:

1) shape   *stave*
2) sound   *song*
3) meaning   *rune*

These three components can be favorably compared to the operant tantric ideology which speaks of the principles of *yantra* (visible device), *mantra* (audible vehicle), and *tantra* (the teaching concerning the meaning and use of things).

In presenting a Transformational Theory of the Word, something must be said about prejudices. In general it may be said that we experience what we expect in life. Expecting Mystery certainly helps to penetrate the veil of prejudice— of using preconceived notions to interpret all of our experiences in day to day life.

Verbal magic, galdor, reorganizes the structure of our expectations. It regularizes magic in our lives— or can do so if we allow/Will it.

Metagenetic memory is stimulated by Runic symbols [the entire complex of shape/sound/meaning], and thereby they are able to re-Call the contents of Deep-Memory. The level of intensity of this re-Call is dependent on the *passion*; the level of precision of the re-Call is dependent on the *accuracy* of the usage of the symbols. *This principle is at the root of why I hold it to be so important to be historically accurate in the use of Runic symbols by today's would-be Runers.* My insistence on accuracy does not come from a pedantic tendency, but rather from a desire to see the Runes become as powerful as possible in today's world.

It must be said that we in the Gild do not seek to transform the world in the image of the ancient world, but rather we seek to transform it according to the archetype of the ancient *ideal* which is entirely without bounds as to time or place.

The greatest Work of Galdor (Rune-Magic) is the Awakening of the Deep-Memory of Runic Knowledge / Understanding and the subsequent actualization of the contents of that Deep-Memory.

The Work of the present-day Runer, and more specifically of the present-day Rune-Master, is no different from that of the ancient Rune-master: to awaken the rulership of the *ginnregin* ("magical gods/advisors") in Midgard. The term *ginnregin* is a technical Icelandic one. It occurs on older runestones, when referring to the source or origin of the Runes themselves, and continues to be used in the *Edda* to designate the Gods in their capacity as inFormers of the human intellect and spirit.

One of the most direct ways in which to do this kind of Work is to engage in the Form of certain key Rune-magical word-formulas.

By *accurately* making (carving or writing) and speaking the formulas:

ᚱᚢᚾᚨ   *rúna*
ᚠᚢᚦᚨᚱᚲ   *futhark*
ᚨᛚᚢ   *alu*

certain pathways can be opened in the inner and outer realms. I invite all readers to engage in the experiment. Be prepared for the consequences as you continue to *reyna til runa*!

RÛNA-Talk I
June 6, 1991ev

The Words and the Word: Auxiliary Formulæ

The reason the Word is "RÛNA," and the reason it has the form it does is simply based on the fact that this is the form in which I Heard the Word. (See RÛNA-Talk O)

This does not end a Mystery but begins to shape many more as we delve deeper into the Word. The reason it was Heard in the form "RÛNA" was a foreshadowing of the form necessary to the completion of the formulaic phrase: *reyn til runa!* In isolation the word *runa* could be taken as the Primitive Norse form of the Proto-Germanic root word: *rūnō*, from which all other historical forms of the word in all the Germanic languages are derived.

RÛNÔ is the Word Heard and Uttered by Wōðanaz— as the divine archetype of the inspired psyche itSelf. My own Understanding has been added to the long and expansive string of articulations of the Word in the interpretive and operative formulas which define the concept as it is to be understood today: "Sense of the Hidden," and which provide the operative key: *"Reyn til Rúna!"*

In a discussion held with Michael Aquino in late October 1988 in Toronto, Canada, as I was first coming to grips with the actualization of the initiatory model provided for within the Temple of Set known as the Fifth Degree, a number of words arose. Among these were "runes" and "troth." Even at that moment, however, the Word RÛNA was clear in my mind, because it is the Word which I Heard, and thus it is the only one I can Utter.

Subsequent to this discussion, however, one of the Nine Unknown appeared to me in a dream— and questioned me as to why the Word was not FUTHARK, one which seemed to make more sense to him.

Only some years later have I come to consider the importance of some of these lexical formulas to the Word RÛNA. Each has its part to play in the mosaic of etymons which reveal and conceal the Rune.

The Rune is the internal (subjective) seed of the ultimate (final) objective psychic reality. The noetic apprehension of the reality and authenticity or viability of the individuated (isolate) principle of the Rune in the individual is the attaining of a state which is neither objective (divorced from individuality) nor subjective (divorced from external reality) but omnijective— a synthetic stasis/dynamis consisting of both poles of this field. From all this the formula "Sense of the Hidden" can be derived, and from it all this verbiage can be delineated.

The words "troth," "futhark" and "alu" are in fact auxiliary formulae to the central formula: RÛNA.

TROTH

"Troth" descends from the Proto-Germanic word *triggwitō*, and is derived from the Indo-European stem *dreu-*, which indicates something "hard, firm, steadfast." It gives us both our words for "tree," and "truth." In connection with RÛNA the auxiliary formula Troth indicates that the path of the discovery of the Unknown and Mysterious requires loyalty to others on the path— an inter-psychic net-work is Necessary. Further, the formula indicates the Necessity of a steadfastness of purpose and Will. In the realm of the Unknown distractions and blind-alleys are commonplace— to find one's way the chief inner tool is that of Troth— of the constancy of the North Star.

FUTHARK

On an outer level the formula FUTHARK is essential. It is the logical and rational *ordering* of elements (the Runes). The formula FUTHARK is a classic *pars pro toto* for the entirety of the Rune-Row. It inspires and directs us to inquire into the objective foundations of things and to discover the secrets contained in such objective foundations. The formula of Reawakening, or the Polarian Method, is based on the formula FUTHARK. This is a chief building block of all my Work:

- objective investigation
- subjective synthesis
- **rea**lization

The FUTHARK system itself is a hallmark of this method. (This is why occultnik rune-kooks just can't seem to get the most basic lore right.)

FUTHARK is the Watch-Word of the Outer Runes— the objective mysteries, which when properly applied, lead to inner revelations.

ALU

Alu, the numerical value of which is 27 = 3 x 9, is the formula of inspired or spiritual order/disorder. This order in disorder is a characteristic of *ginnung*, the "magically charged void" out of which the world is first given shape. This is the root of pure power and contact with it effects the experience of inspiration (ON *óðr*)— and even madness if it is not rightly tempered with the FUTHARK formula. ALU exhorts us to explore the subjective universe of the mind and soul, and to discover its secrets.

ALU is the Watch-Word of the Inner Runes— the subjective mysteries, which when properly applied, unravel the riddle of the world.

* *
*

To summarize: The Rune is the Goal of the Search, the Search must be True and so too the Searcher; FUTHARK shows the Way and ALU gives the Power.

EΩA

RÚNA-Talk II
June 15, 1991ev

The Polarian Method and RÚNA

In the last talk I alluded to a "Polarian Method." Here we will explore this idea further.

Óðinn is the God of polarities. He balances any and all polar opposites by indulging in the extremes of each end of the spectrum. By oscillating between these extremes a dynamic balance is achieved which no other method is capable of achieving.

This method is applied to the greater Workings of RÚNA as follows. The greater Workings of RÚNA are aimed at achieving certain Willed aims in the subjective universes of individual Runers, as well as effecting certain Willed changes in the objective universe in harmony with the transformed souls of the Runers.

The first element or component in this method is a subjective (inner) Passion for a given Work or activity. Upon this depends the intensity or pure *power* of the results which might be gained. The beginnings of this factor lies in the first principle of all philosophy: a Sense of Wonder (Aristotle). There must be an inspirational *charge* to the Work. Galdor-Work is not mere dispassionate science— the spiritual enthusiasm is an important factor in the process. This is why mere "scientific methods" are impotent when trying to unravel the mysteries of the universe.

This passion-factor, the intensity of emotion attached to certain thoughts and ideas, is really quite common, most especially in the "occultnik" world. Enthusiasm, at least an enthusiasm which will last as long as it takes to buy into the next occult fashion or craze, is in abundant supply. This enthusiasm is usually very short lived, however, because it is running on external and inauthentic fuel. This serves the commercial purveyors of the "mysteries" just fine because they are excused from having to reveal the ultimate Mysteries by simply having you move onto the next phase or craze. So the typical occultnik goes through life skipping from phase to phase— like a flat rune-cookie over the surface of a tranquil lake.

What is usually lacking among occultniks is the objective (outer) Precision for a given Work or activity. This factor is essential because upon it is dependent the accuracy of the results which might be gained. This is the realm of hard work and discipline— things which many in the "occult world" got into that very world to avoid. Although many will see the Precision-factor as "elitist," in fact it is the opposite. Inspiration comes only to the few, but virtually all can be taught to use precise tools for self-improvement. Some can make great progress with enthusiasm alone (combined with luck and/or the *gebō/naupiz* [*grace*] of a God), but this is rare. More can make some progress applying definite and precise instructions.

The maximal power, however, is to be gained by the extreme and balanced application of *both* factors simultaneously.

To summarize: in a formula wherein we allow a = (subjective) Passion of the work and b = (objective) Precision of the work: a x b = Power of Result.

The enthusiasm is the power of the bow and the arm that draws it, while the accuracy is in the craftsman and the shooter who aims the arrow. All factors are necessary to hit the target and win the day.

Certainly a balance between Passion and Precision, Enthusiasm and Accuracy must be sought and maintained. This is yet another example of the Germanic path being one that cuts between extremes— not only by negating both (as one might find in Buddhistic schools) or by exhalation one over the other (as might be found in Gnostic ones)— but by seeking the depths of each extreme and thereby ensuring the dynamism and power of the resulting balance in motion.

Balance is much easier to maintain when in motion rather than while being still. Notice when you ride a bicycle: when in forward motion balance comes naturally, while only an acrobat has an easy time staying balanced and upright on a motionless bike. The point of Rune-Work is to develop Self, not to get a job in the circus.

RÚNA as an Ideogrammic Formula

The Runes have often been read as pure ideograms, and there is ample evidence for this level of their understanding in the oldest of sources. When we apply an ideogramic reading to the Word RÚNA, the following results can be derived:

RÚNA = ᚱ = a rational measured tradition of right
ᚢ = empowered by "going under" to the depths of life and death
ᚾ = tested by crisis and need
ᚠ = emerging in the consciousness and inspiration of the gods

Thus the Word teaches us about itself from within itself according to its own frames of reference. In this ideogramic formula RÚNA speaks to some nuances of the Passion : Precision formula already discussed. She teaches us, however, in her own mysterious way— and I can only urge you to listen.

Reyn til Rúna as a Numerical Formula

It may be noted that when the Icelandic phrase *reyn til rúna* is transliterated accurately into the runes of the younger futhark, the precise futhark system into which it should be transliterated, and which is precisely most suited to its expression, the following formula results:

ᚱᛁᚾ   ᛏᛁᛚ   ᚱᚢᚾᛅ

In the tally-lore, or numerology, of the runes, when the numerical value of each of these younger staves is added together to yield a sum, the following can be discovered:

ᚱᛁᚾᛏᛁᛚᚱᚢᚾᛅ
5.10.9.8.12.9.15.5.2.8.10 = 93

Those who have studied the Word of Will shall at once make note that the key-number of *thelêma*, derived from the gematric sum of the Greek word θελημα, is also 93. This reveals the hidden link between *thelêma* and RÛNA, and at once indicates the mode by which the Work of *thelêma* is best projected forward.

EΩA

RÛNA-Talk III
June 30, 1991ev

Universalizing the System

Shortly before I gave this talk, I heard the call to Universalize my System. This had in part been the purpose of the RÛNA-Talks, but at the same time my field of vision had been narrow, and had not expanded beyond those who had the capability of grasping the essence of the Mystery. But really all can benefit from the RÛNA-system on a certain level.

In the simplest terms, the system can be expressed in the ASA-Formula: Awaken, See, and Act. The same principles at work in the Polarian Method are present here.

AWAKEN
SEE
ACT

These are three parts of a greater whole. One action is not to be undertaken without the others. Each is to proceed in its right order.

To Awaken is to see life and the environment with new eyes and a new perspective. You are moving through life as a sleep-walker. You are only aware of those things which you have been trained to be aware of— ideas which have been rendered forbidden or tabu by your peer-group and environment have been filtered out. Seek a moment of Awakening— expect it every morning, expect it every day, expect it every moment of your life, whether your body is asleep or awake.

It will take some time of living with such expectation of Awakening before you have really been able to shake yourself into a fairly consistent state of mindfulness. Most would count such an Awakening as a great accomplishment. It is not— not in and of itself. One can become virtually addicted to these moments of Awakening. They feel good. But they only serve to open a door. Without them no further progress is possible, but they are not an end in themselves.

The next stage is to See— that is to understand and comprehend what is in front of your Awakened eye. The process of Awakening is an influx of energy, the process of Seeing is the direction of that energy to the essential task of *orienting* one's self on a path of development. Where am I? Where do I want to go? Who am I? Who do I want to be? These questions can not be reliably posed, much less answered in a Sleeping state, so Awakening comes before Seeing. (Seeing in the Sleeping state is tantamount to dreaming.)

Finally the greatest task is to ACT— actually do something based on the answers to the questions you have posed to yourSelf in the Awakened state. Surely no one who has Awakened in the light of RÛNA, and who has posed the Questions in that light will have answers which are other than the most *noble* and *heroic* answers possible for that person at that time. Not every one will have the same answers, because no two persons are the same or equal. What the answers will share is the level of *quality* measured against the absolute potential of the given individual.

ACTION is something others can see. We live in Midgard — action-central of the world order — for a reason. We are here to ACT, and in acting to elevate our BEING. Real Knowledge leads to Action, and Action to evolution of Self.

*   *
*

Another factor which I might venture here is that the Way of Woden, although best expressed in terms of the Germanic tradition to which it belongs and out of which it grows, nevertheless can be universalized in a sense. One does not need to use the name of Woden or the symbolism of the Runes to gain the initiatory benefits the archetype and paradigm of development can offer. The structures involved are unique and might be applied independently of the symbols. In fact I prefer it to be the case with most individuals who are not committed to the Way of Woden that they not use the symbols of that Way if they are not *committed* to it. However, learning the principles of the Way and applying them apart from the symbols can be a source of great reward for those who are unwilling, or unable due to prior commitments in life, to Give themSelves not only to themSelves, but also to the goals of the Great Tradition.

RÛNA-Talk IV
July 6, 1991ev

Head Staves

I

I introduce this talk with some material from Mircea Eliade's *History of Religious Ideas*, volume I, pp. 300-301:

> The religious, and in general, the cultural value of "secrecy" has as yet been inadequately studied. All the great discoveries and inventions — agriculture, metallurgy, various techniques, arts, etc. — implied, in the beginning, secrecy, for it was only those "initiated" into the secrets of the craft who were believed able to guarantee the success of the operation. With time, initiation into the arcana of certain archaic techniques became accessible to the whole community. However, the various techniques did not entirely lose their sacred character...

Eliade goes on to explain the quality of secrecy in the process of "revelation":

> Now such revelations demanded secrecy as a condition *sine qua non*. The procedure was the same in the various initiations documented in archaic societies. What is unique about the Eleusian secrecy is the fact that it became a paradigmatic model for Mystery cults. The religious value of secrecy will be extoled in the Hellenistic period. The mythologization of initiatory secrets and their hermeneutics will later encourage countless speculations, which will end by shaping the style of the whole period. "Secrecy even increases the value of what is learned," writes Plutarch (*On the Life and Poetry of Homer* 92). Medicine and philosophy are both held to possess initiatory secrets which different authors compare to aspects of Eleusis. In the days of the Neo-Pythagoreans and Neo-Platonists, one of the cliche's most employed was precisely the enigmatic style of the great philosophers, the idea that the masters revealed their true doctrine only to initiates.

Those who Know also Know the perspective from which Eliade spoke.

II

Head-Staves

1. The world is a building of the Mind through the Ages, these buildings are other worlds, or realms of being, and becoming— each of which is ruled by its own head-stave or first-form. Knowledge of the character of this head-stave is the key which unlocks its rune or mystery.

2. Beyond all single manifestations of such worlds and runes stands *the* Rune (RÛNA) from which all others are derived.

3. Because it is the very essence of the Unknown or Hidden, it shall remain forever Unknown and Hidden.

4. The proof of the power of Rúna is not in the amount of Truth it reveals upon its Hearing, but the amount of Work or activity generated by the Quest for it.

5. One of the keys to the use of RÛNA is the ability to harness and direct the energy released by its Knowledge in a Willed way in accordance with one's Needs for Becoming.

III

This RÛNA-Talk was concluded with a further numerological exploration of the formula: *Reyn til Rúna* (= 5.10.9.8.12.9.14.5.2.8.10 = 93). The bindrune of the formula:

is, of course, made up of a combination of the three Runestaves R+T+R (= 5.12.5 = 22 = 2 x 11, which might also be expressed 11/11. Its link with the traditions of the Temple of Set will be known to some, but more to the point it is an analysis of the *Ingwaz*-character of the formula as an eternally gestating and transformative seed-form— a kernel that when split yields two shining swords of Ice (*îsa*). The dynamic is made static and stable in the perfected *ego* (*ek*) of Man.

These and many other revelations in tally-lore, or numerology, have been made in connection with RÛNA. A word must be said on the value of such things. In operative or speculative runology *number* is not so much a matter of quantity as it is a *quality*. Typically, and as we have come to expect when dealing with RÛNA, reality is often not what it at first appears. Number *per sé* as a symbol partakes of the analytical and objective faculties. We know well that the ancient skalds carefully counted syllables in their poetry, and the renowned Norwegian runologist Magnus Olsen even showed how the rune-counts could be reconstructed for the poetry of Egill Skallagrimsson. Number has power as a consciously applied, *poetic* technique. Numerical patterns make the Work more powerful by making it more harmonious with its aim. On the other hand, when *discovering* implicit and latent patterns and potencies in pre-existing formulas, not consciously created to fulfill a numerical pattern — such as is the case with the *reyn til runa* formula — the power is in the pure joy (*wunjō*) of the discovery. The wonder and astonishment at the moment of the intersection of knowledge and paradigm *is* the essence of the "message." Over-use (i.e. *mis*-use) of such patterns are counterproductive to the process.

RÛNA-Talk O
July 18, 1991ev

Transformation and RÛNA

To begin with we must ask: What is "transformation"?

It is simply, yet profoundly, the movement of essence from one form to another: In galdor-work, or magic, this is the movement from a base form to a Willed target-form which has definite characteristics.

There are may kinds of Transformation: The two principal kinds are:

1) One with a *known*, or conscious, target-form. This kind of transformation is a (re-)shaping of pre-existing Form, and is the only type of "creation" possible.

2) One with an *unknown*, or unconscious, target-form— that is the subject (doer) of the transformation is in the beginning unaware or unconscious of the final Form which the transformation will take. This is the process of *discovery* of unknown factors.

The former kind of Transformation is straightforward and requires strength of Will, the latter is mysterious and relies on the precision of the method employed.

<u>The target must not be perfect, but the way must be.</u>

A second question arises: Is Transformation always "positive," that is, *beneficial* to the subject?

The answer to this question is an unqualified "no."

All transformation *must* be is *change*. How that change manifests may be beneficial or detrimental, or neutral to the development and even happiness of the subject.

A third question arises for those in the School of XEPER, and in essence for all dedicated to Self-development: Is XEPER Transformation?

Again the answer is "no" because XEPER is the Becoming of Being, of Essence, of Consciousness, not merely "change for the sake of change.

How is this Self-Development Willed?

You must gain Knowledge and Experience (action). The combination of these results in the Evolution of Being. Only with this evolved Being is Understanding possible, and only with Understanding is the formulation of precise target- forms possible in the practice of *Transformational Magic*.

Experience (Action) comes on many levels: but the *physical* is most noble (for at that level the greatest resistance is offered). The principle of Resistance is essential in development. Note how the bodybuilder uses gravity and weight to develop muscle. Resistance is directly translated into development. This is true on all levels. Only hard things are worth doing. If it's not hard, you're working on the wrong thing.

Knowledge also comes on many levels: (minds, hearts, bodies) but the intellectual and verbal/mathematical is the most noble of these levels because it is at that level that the greatest precision is possible.

It must also be remembered that *both* physical and intellectual Action and Knowledge are Necessary to the entire process of Self-development.

Another questions arises: How can we Willfully direct Transformation?

Step *toward* the Willed Form— but then, at the last moment, step a bit to the side of it to Become that which *you are*, not that which *it* (the artificial target-form) is, or that which you *thought* you were.

What is the role of RÛNA in Transformation?

RÛNA is Necessary to *true* Transformation in consciousness because if you already knew and understood the parameters of the "target-form" you would essentially BE there already— no *real* Transformation would have taken place. Nor would it have been Necessary. Nevertheless, even in this process you will certainly have raised yourself to a higher "octave."

There must always, by Necessity, be an element of the Hidden in the process of true Transformation.

I will leave you with this meditational consideration: If you could really change yourself at this moment in time into a Being of your own conscious design— would you do it?

RÛNA-Talk V
August 3, 1991ev

Is RÛNA for All?

Of course, the title of this talk is a play off of the book title by Aleister Crowley: *The Law is for All*. Crowley, as a typical *modern* believed in the universal application of "magical" principles in a manner analogous to the application of scientific principles. If a scientific *law*, such as might govern gravity, is valid for all people, then so too must magical laws be valid for all people. The ancients knew this to be false because although the world of nature (and hence of science) is gross and belongs to the lowest common denominator, the psyche is rare and belongs to the uncommon level of experience and reality. Laws valid in the rarified states of the psyche may not be valid in the natural world. Although the wise might be able to read the secret correspondences and analogies between the two worlds, the *ways* the "laws" behave within the two worlds have more that separates them than holds them together.

Contrary to what occult publishers might want you to believe, "magic" is not for all, "magic" is not the "easiest and most natural thing in the world"— it is the hardest and most non-natural thing.

Nevertheless, we might answer the question as to whether RÛNA is for all in the affirmative— if only on a highly qualified basis. All do indulge in the sense of the unknown which drives their curiosity even on the most mundane of affairs: "Is she *really* a redhead?" "Who shot J.R?" There is an inner sense of curiosity which is the driving force for most of human activity— and in this way RÛNA is experienced by *all* humans on a fairly frequent basis. It is on the inner or subjective level where most people experience at least the shadow or reflection of RÛNA most regularly.

On another level the answer to the question is negative— only a very *few* will ever be *called* to Quest for the unknown in the objective sense. This call comes in the form of a manifestation of the Sense of the absolute Unknown having its origins in the outer, objective universe. Its source is *the* Rune, RÚNA. For the many the phenomena created by the issuance of this call from RÚNA to the few is an unending source of fear and hatred. Only the elite few can confront the Unknown and be inspired and motivated by it— the many fear and hate the unknown, that which they do not (and in most instances *cannot* understand. In Jungian psychology the manifestation of such patterns are well-known in the phenomenon of the *shadow*.

I am reminded here of a moment in my first graduate lecture in diachronic (historical) linguistics taught by my *Doktorvater*, Edgar Polomé. At one point he wrote some word in Greek (and with the Greek alphabet) on the board, turned to the students and, with a perfectly straight face, said: "You all know Greek, *don't you*?" Then as he turned back to the board, there was a slight trace of his endearing smile. That was an initiatory moment. At that moment, the "students" could go one of two ways in their minds. One group, the majority, would think: "Who does this guy think he is! I'm a German major! He's making me feel dumb! I don't like it!" While another group, much smaller, indeed, thought: "I should learn Greek." Or at least: "It sure would be good if I knew Greek." The many will feel outraged and "belittled." The few will feel challenged and even inspired. Thus is the effect of certain remarkable men.

* * *
* *

There is an Old Norse word which answers to the sound of the Word perfectly. This is *Rúna*. It means (feminine) "secret advisor." There is also a masculine form of the word: *Rúni*, which means (masculine) "secret advisor." In an esoteric sense this is the "one who whispers in your ear." This is always an erotically symbolic entity— and is usually perceived as a contra-sexual being. That is, for men it usually is seen as a female being, for women a male one. This is part of your soul— but a part of it which is always urging you to evolve to a higher level and Become. The reason for this is that she (or he) is lonely and you can only be reunited with her (or him) once you become a part of her (or his) world. This unseen accompanying spirit is the eternally transformative presence of RÚNA in your life. In a sense this is an inner partner and advisor on the Runic Way.

This pattern is seen in the world of Gods as well as divine heroes. For Óðinn this is *Rúna* herself, the first Rune, who he took up screaming at his initial initiation into the Runes. She may also be known as Hulda, the Hidden One, or on another level as "the Lady"— Freyja. In a sense this feminine counterpart is the Hidden soul of the God.

In the same way the *valkyrja* Sigrdrífa (or Brunnhildr) is this for the ultimate hero Sigurðr. It is interesting to note that the element *sigr-* is developed in these names: Sigrdrífa means "she who *drives* or leads victory," while Sigurðr means "he who guards victory." She is the dynamic motivator, he is the static manifestation. She is the power, he is the power-holder. EΩA

So, there is an inner *Rúna*, who is a driver or motivator of the Quest. On occasion in the past I have given this entity the name or title the "Transformatrix." (Transform-Matrix!) the sense of an inner being of the opposite sex which is inborn, innate. Goethe recognized this principle of the feminine in the final lines of his monumental *Faust II*, when the old magician, who is about to be drug to Hell, is inexplicably saved by the power and grace of *das Ewig Weibliche* ("the Eternal Feminine"), which, Goethe put it, *zieht uns immer hinan—* draws us ever onward.

Remarkably and miraculously, this inner *Rúna* — for some who find themselves on the Quest — will be found in the outer world in fleshly form. The *Rúna* (or *Rúni*) will often be found in the most unlikely of places— but always at the most likely of *times* in the Life-Quest of the Runer.

This pattern of erotically paired individuals who fulfil the roles of the *Magus* and his "Scarlet Woman" is found in the magical mythologies of many peoples. Most notably this is a prominent feature of the Hermeto-Gnostic schools of the

Hellenistic world. We need think only of the relationship of Jesus, Magus and his Mary Magdalene, or most pointedly of Simon, Magus and his Helena.

RÛNA-Talk VI
August 10, 1991ev

RÛNA and *WYRD*

This talk is really an exercise in the use of the verbal concept contained within RÛNA. What does it mean "to rune" something. At first glance of course this makes no sense, because the word "rune" itself cannot be used as a verb. But the stem-form did develop verbal usages. In (Old) English we have the verb, *rûnian*: 'to whisper.' The verb "to roun," also meaning "whisper" and "pass secret information" has also survived in some English usage. Most importantly, however, we discover the verbal use of the concept with the Icelandic word *reyna*, 'to try; to experience; to examine; to search or pry (into), with *eptir* or *til*.' (See Cleasby-Vigfusson, *An Icelandic-English Dictionary*, p. 496.)

As I "runed" the Word/concept of Becoming in a Germanic context I came to recognize that the root concept of Becoming in Germanic was linked to our modern word "weird." For purposes of clarity, I spell the word anachronistically as /wyrd/. Wyrd is derived from the Old English verb *weorðan*, 'to become; turn.' This word has largely fallen out of modern English usage. However, in Icelandic its full implications are clear: There we discover the word *urðr*, which is formed from the plural past tense stem of the verb *verða*, 'to become'— the exact cognate of OE *weorðan*. *Urðr*, according to Cleasby-Vigfusson, means 'a weird, fate.'

Etymologically the word means "that which has become," or that which turned (out)." This is, of course, also the name of the first Norn: *Urðr*. The second Norn is called *Verðandi*, whose name is simply the present participle of the same verb, with the general meaning "that which is becoming," or "that which (at the present moment) is turning (out)." To the speakers of ancient, as well as modern Germanic dialects, such as English, there are apparently only two *real* times: the Past, which is *objective reality*, and the Present, which is a fleeting moment, but an immediate reality.

41

The word "weird," by the way has a lively set of meanings in the Scots dialect of English. In Warrack's *Scots Dialect Dictionary* we read:

> Weird, n. a fateful being; a dealer in the supernatural; disaster; a fateful story; a prediction, prophesy.— v. to doom to; to adjure by the knowledge of impending fate; to predict; to waft kind wishes; to make liable to; to expose to evil.

Delving below the surface we discover that WYRD has two distinct aspects:

The first aspect indicates that what is WYRD has its origins in what is **objectively** (even if *mythically* or *ideally*) **real**. This refers to the fact that what is WYRD has come into being, is stable and relatively fixed— however, it is hidden from our view. It is only accessible through myth (story-telling or "history") or in moments of extraordinary conscious clarity. These moments can be reached through Rune-Work, or completely by accident.

This aspect of WYRD is in stark contrast to the experience of the present moment, which is an intense singular focus (whereas the realm of WYRD is a whole expansive sea of Being) and in contrast to the "non-present" reality of things which have not (yet) happened, which is a sea of fluid and unstable possibilities which are in constant flux. WYRD is the only power which can bring this instability into stability— which it consistently and naturally tends to do. Hence the realization that what is "weird" is something which will affect or shape the "future."

The other aspect of WYRD is its meaning which indicates the whole *process* of "becoming." Here WYRD is the *form* or *principle* of "process" itself. This archetypal meaning is etymologically conveyed by the fact that the word is formed from the past participle of the verb "to become." Hence it is "the past" as the mythically or ideally true or real.

One way to "rune" (rown) the concept /wyrd/ is to practice Runic (or other forms of) "divination." In so doing one explores the "past" as something which conditions, or even, in extreme cases, determines what will happen in the "future." But remember, such divination is *not* an investigation of the "future" because strictly speaking it does not exist, but rather a rationally intuitive investigation of the patterns of the past which will give rise to patterns of the "future."

One should explore one's own mythic and historical past. What stories about your family provided the family "mythology." What does your genealogical record indicate? The discovery of one's genealogy is tantamount to the discovery of your own family saga. The Icelandic sagas were not originally "history" so much as they were mythicizations of the families. Due to their (our) kind of belief in "reincarnation" these sagas served as "past life regressions." Except they were far more reliable and objective.

One should also explore one's own personal past. Review both life and the mythos about your life, and in all instances apply the Runic Test— Ask the Question: What is *hidden* here? What is the unspoken secret which explains this or that event? Be strong when you enter this realm. Be prepared for some shocks when RÛNA begins to speak to you directly.

So, how is RÛNA related to WYRD? RÛNA is a sense of the hidden (within and without) of every **subject** of the process of *Becoming* (that is, WYRD). This RÛNA acts as a motivator of Becoming. It is the mo**ver** and dynami**zer** of the process of Becoming, the secret of which is WYRD. This process is made conscious in the Runer by the formula *reyn til rúna*!

So *Wyrd* is first the principle of becoming (= the "idealized past"), and second the process of becoming in action.

When we *sense* or perceive the otherwise hidden reality of this process we perceive a certain *weirdness* (wyrdness). This is an extra-ordinarily meaningful experience which is tinged with a sense of connection with a *hidden* or *Runic* world.

It is in just such moments when the sense of the present moment (Verðandi) and the eternally meaningful, yet ever extraordinary, realm of Wyrd (*Urðr*) intersect that were first interpreted as the experience of the "weird."

RÛNA-Talk VII
August 24, 1991ev

Modeling and Re-Modeling of Self and Culture

In following the formula of *Reyn til Rúna*, the use of a doctrine of models is of extreme importance. Models, or exemplary models, are conscious constructs by which Runers seek to form and re-form not only the personality, but also their very essence of Being.

There are essentially four types of such models: the divine (or archetypal), the heroic, and the human, which is further subdivided into historical figures and individuals actually known to a person:

1. Divine/Archetypal
2. Heroic
3. Human a) Historical
4.   b) Personally Known

This forms a sort of "periodic table" of exemplary models, because each type has its special uses, and each is distinct from the others according to a formula of distinctive features.

The divine exemplary model can never be "attained," nor does the Runer strive to do so. The Runer can only strive *toward* this exemplary model, which is like unto the Grail, ever sought but never gained. The effects of the influx of inFormation from such divine exemplary models is usually quite subtle. Drastic breakthroughs of the forms of these models is dramatic and often chaos inducing. Óðinn is the perfect exemplary model on the divine level for Runers, although some also see Freyja in this light. These are the Gods and Goddesses of various national pantheons.

More suited to direct modeling are the heroic forms. A hero is a figure who is definitely *human* (although the figure may be seen as the son or daughter of a divinity). In any event, the hero is seen as *human*, and hence faces *human* problems.

For this reason they exist, and in this way the Runer can more directly model mental forms on such heroes. The most prominent such heroes for the Runer is Sigurðr Fáfnisbani.

Distinguished from the great heroes from the purely mythic realm by their historicity (portrayal in more Midgard-bound time/space) are heroes such as Egill Skallagrimsson. These are men and women who walked the same Midgard in which we exist, and who worked great deeds, worthy of our emulation. They provide more "realistic" goals of actual Midgard-bound achievements toward which to strive. (Usually authors of books which have greatly influenced us belong to this category—until we perhaps meet and get to know them as real people.)

Finally there are those "role models" who we have known and who have played roles in our development: our parents, some teachers, friends, and so on. These are the direct guides of our behavior (consciously or unconsciously). The keys to the understanding of role models in our lives are 1) to recognize this type of model's continuity with, yet distinction from the three other kinds of models, and 2) to be consciously aware of the patterns being imparted by such role models. Seek models which are in harmony with your goals and *cause* them to have maximal impact on you. Once you have learned their lessons, you can re-synthesize what you have learned to shape a higher form of Being from your experience. This is just one of the traditional ways such modeling can be used, and for centuries has been used, to effect Self-Transformation.

Almost all of human behavior, and all of culture, is based on *contact* between and among human beings. When we speak of culture we are speaking of four distinct, yet interrelated areas:

CULTURE

Ethnic (Racial)	Ethical (Ideological)
Material	Linguistic

We can speak of "ethnic culture"— which is predicated on sexual contact leading to the reproduction of the human bodies which literally *embody* the culture. We can speak of "ethical culture" which is the totality of the symbolic or idea-content of the intellectual life of the culture. This would include the ideological contents of its religion(s), philosophies, political systems, economic systems, and so on. Thus we see the dichotomy between the material and the intellectual. This pattern is continued as we observe the idea of "material culture." This is all the actual concrete *objects* which the culture creates: its buildings, clothing, vehicles, furniture— all the *physical* objects which it might leave behind in an archeological record. Finally there is "linguistic culture." This is the encoding of its ideas in symbolic forms which make them communicable both within the culture, and which make it at least partially possible for those outside the culture to understand some of it— if the code is known. Again we note how there is a dichotomy between the material on the left side of the chart, and the symbolic on the right.

Taken all together these form the entirety of what a whole culture is about. All four areas must be considered, all four areas are essential to the existence and continuity of a culture.

A culture is an organic, communal individuality. As each *individual* human being possesses a body and thoughts, as each individual makes things and puts things together, and as each individual has a unique symbolic way of expressing him or herself— so too does a collective body of individuals who share a certain level of genetic material, share certain ideas and values given shape by their language and common sense of the æsthetic. Such is a Nation. And it is in a Nation where Man finds his Natural home.

The Runic tradition addresses itself to the idea of *culture* on many occasions and in many ways. *Gebō*: 'the gift', embodies how two individuals *exchange* something in order to build a bond. *Wunjō*: 'joy' shows the result of harmonious actions of humans working in cooperation, while *ōpila*, 'ancestral property', is the profound mystery of *heritage*: what is inherited from one generation to the next in the eternal chain of cultural contact. The very *subject* of culture is, however, *mannaz*: 'the human being.' The Icelandic term for "culture" is *menning*, which in the old language was synonymous with "breeding." But etymologically it is derived from the stem *mann-*, through the verbal form *menna*: 'to educate into a human being.' Truths were built right into the old languages, stemming from ideological knowledge proven by material experience which all our politicians and educators have either forgotten or set out (unconsciously, and hence most dangerously) to destroy.

In "runing" the idea of *culture* we must seek the *hidden* principles underlying the true nature of the individual and understand the degree to which each individual is the product of inter-relationships with other individuals over vast expanses of time, and how individuals can compete and/or cooperate in order to bring about an elevation in the level of quality in a given culture.

Far from bringing war and conflict, the ultimate blooming of the Runic flower will bring "peace." Because as individuals must be "individuated" in order to become happy and whole, so too must collective bodies of individuals (Nations). It is the destructive force of the thurses which demand unanimity and "one-ness"— but under whose set of values? Under those of the thurs-forces, of course.

The role of the Runic movement in culture in the world today is only now in its (second) embryonic stage. The prospects for its ultimate birth are questionable, because the ideas inherent in it are the target of all the unconscious forces of ignorance and stupidity (thurs-forces). If, however, the Runic message can be *Heard*, the prospects for true frith and grith in the world will be unparalleled.

Exemplary models — patterns or paradigms — of being and behavior must be used both individually and culturally on a wider level in order to effect transformations in the individual Self and in the culture.

RÛNA-Talk VIII
August 31, 1991ev

RÛNA as a Trans-Æonic Word

RÛNA

In a continuation of some of the ideas brought up in RÛNA-Talk VI, it is essential to understand the essence of RÛNA as a Word, as a concept, which transcends the order of worlds, or *æons*.

Because RÛNA *is* the Hidden its very existence gives rise to a "sense" — or intuition — of the Hidden in any conscious being. This is the first moment of great Inspiration (*wôð; óðr*) in the first model of *human* consciousness— known in the Germanic Tradition, which places this entity at the center of its mythology, as Óðinn.

The *factum* ("done-deal") of the existence of an **opposite** hidden within the principle of intelligence precedes (comes before) the sense — or intuition. This moment of inspiration and realization is then developed by the principle of intelligence into the idea that there is in fact something hidden— which a fully conscious being reacts to by seeking to discover the mystery. Therefore from the principle of the Hidden, the exhortation to "seek the mystery" is automatic in the environment of intelligence.

Worlds / Aiōns

The doctrine of worlds holds that there emanates from a primeval oneness — or wholeness — a multiplicity of interlocked and inter-related cycles of becoming and levels of being. These were known to the Greeks (Hermetics and Gnostics) as æons (Gk. αιωνες), and to the Germanic peoples as worlds (ON *veraldar*) or "homes" (ON *heimar*). The Germanic term "world" is derived etymologically from stems which indicate that the original term meant "the age of (a) man." Therefore it is linked to the idea of time/space and to the psyche (which is what makes a Man). Of course, to the

Kabbalist each of these emanations is called a (Heb.) *sefirah*, derived from the Greek term σφαιρα: 'sphere'.

There is much misunderstanding as to the true nature of time. We are tricked by our often limited perspective on life into thinking that we are locked into a progressive linear time model: past-present-future. The influence of Classical grammar and Judeo-Christian mythology have tainted our Germanic view of time: "past" (= ideal reality), "present" (= moment of absolute freedom) and "non-past" (= potential action conditioned/determined by the "past").

In fact, for us, the progressive ages of linear time are a misinterpretation of an eternal dynamism. Progress in technology can be measured in linear terms— but not the (illusory) "progress" of mankind. Perhaps we can build better and better machines, so that our weapons are 2,000 times more destructive than the weapons of 2,000 years ago— but are our philosophies 2,000 times better? Are we 2,000 times more advanced as human beings than we were, as a species, 2,000 years ago. I don't think so.

The belief that Mankind is progressing as a species in linkage with his technological (scientific) development is the hallmark of what is called "modernism."

In reality æons are not simply pearls on the string of time. They are not linear, nor are they quantitatively definable in any ontological way. They exist, but their exact character, number and arrangement are in slight flux at all times, in major flux at others.

Aleister Crowley, who popularized the doctrine of Æons for the occultnik world in the 20th century had only a thoroughly modernist and evolutionist attitude toward the doctrine. He essentially used the model which had been developed by Joachim of Fiore concerning the passage of history through three successive "Ages" and applied to it pagan Egyptian symbols rather than the Christian ones used by Joachim. For Joachim it was the Ages of the Father, Son and Holy Ghost, for Crowley these were the Ages of Isis, Osiris and Horus— the Mother-Father-Child. In this model Crowley was, of course, heavily influenced by the modern theories of cultural "evolution" (many of which were Marxist, or used by Marxists) which posited an original communism characterized by matriarchy, which was succeeded in time by property holding culture characterized by patriarchy. All such theories are locked in an unrealistic view of the linearity of time and "history."

In fact we know that the ancient period did not pass away with the Middle Ages (otherwise a Renaissance would be impossible), nor have the Middle Ages left us (just look at cable television). The Ages of human culture are a mosaic of mutually interacting and temporally coexisting dimensions— not material stages of a narrative. This is the heritage of the Old Testament, and is unNecessary.

Crowley's description of Æonic Words, although perhaps pioneering at the time, has long since been superseded. The number of Æons that coexist in the Universe is unknown. Their number is probably not a static one in reality. But it is certain that the historical description championed by Crowley is inaccurate. The reason it may appeal to persons today is merely a reflection of the degree to which Judeo-Christian and modernistic (scientific) paradigms still hold sway in the popular mind.

It must be said that Crowley's Word: *Thelēma*, which he defined as "True Will," was largely taken from the writings of the German philosopher Friedrich Nieztsche, who must be counted as the "proto-Magus" of that Word as it has been playing itself out in the 20th century.

Thus æons are to be seen as dimensions of space/time— not as stages of history.

Operative Uses of Words

To return to the relationship of Words to Worlds, it may be said that each world, or æon, is described by a Word— a conceptual key which also gives the mind access to that World. These Words, like the cycles and levels themselves are not in reality linear constructs in natural languages, but are reflections of eternal archetypes, or seed-words which lie beyond the ability of the five senses to model them.

To be able to "say" one of these Words, that is to Know it *really*, is a matter of being able to Understand it and formulate it within your own mind. The process is dimly reflected in the learning of natural languages, such as we all speak. But it is, however, on a higher level of intellectual task performance, to say the least.

To have it befall one to have to "utter" such a Word, that is to recast it out of the stream of Words in an original way— to give (re-)birth to it is a task fraught with a mighty curse. This is simply because such utterances (original formulations) will come about in times and places where there is an imbalance to the disadvantage of the concept. The Utterer will (re-)introduce the concept to a hostile and fearful World— he or she will usually be martyred (literally or figuratively) for their Works.

The Word (concept) of Becoming (XEPER), Uttered by Michael Aquino in 1975ce — and extended to the Formula, in the Egyptian language, *Xepera-Xeper-Xeperu* — is the Word of Æons. That is, it is the model which makes the actual concept of an Æon real and intelligible. The actual activity of cyclical dynamism is generated by this Formula.

It is said that there are Words which are Æonic, or which "enhance" an Æonic Word, and there are Meta- or Trans-Æonic Words. An Æon is a cycle of time *and* existence. There can also be Words which will enhance or further develop both Æonic and Trans-Æonic Words.

RÛNA is just such a *Trans-Æonic* Word: It is the Mystery [μυστηριον] or Secret [κρυπτον] which lies within and behind humanity's ability to seek and to comprehend a *mystery*, i.e. to know or understand it. Its reality is within humanity and without it.

XEPER, or WYRD, is the Æonic Word of all Æonic Words in that it describes the very essence of *all* cycles that ever have been or that ever will or could be. The entirety of the cyclical pattern could be described as: Manifestation —> Being —> Dismanifestation —> Remanifestation, *et cetera ad infinitum*.

A Trans-Æonic Word, by its very definition, lies *outside* the rings or cycles of the Æons themselves. It lies outside the mosaic of inter-locking models which make up the Æons, or Worlds.

RÛNA is just such a Trans-Æonic Word. RÛNA is the Hidden within the depths of the first principle of isolate intelligence. This principle of isolate intelligence Sensed at once the existence of this Hidden as its first Thought. By the same token the Hidden was given shape and definition by the Thought and responded to the stimulus from the Prince (the First One) and (She) became curious. Thus, with Her curiosity, she began to wander and thus began to "create," give shape to, the worlds or levels of existence.

You can read about similar "psycho-cosmologies" in the writings of the Hermetics, Gnostics, and others of centuries ago.* The same pattern is also clearly present in the poetic renditions found in the *Eddas*.

It is this which is at the root of the mythology of Óðinn's Runic Initiation on the World-Tree, Yggdrasill and his *taking up* of the Hidden in the Form of the Rune (RÛNA), which he is able to Understand, break-down, or analyze into the Runes— the codification of the Mystery in the enumerated and ordered elements which he imparts to mankind in the form of the runestaves.

The link or bond between two extremities lies in the (un)known *sense* of one polar side of a complex concerning the character of its opposite. Each extreme holds the key of its opposite, although because it is deeply buried in the essence of the opposite, it remains hidden, and difficult to unlock.

RÛNA implies the absolute *necessity* of plurality and multiversality: From the Rune came the Runes, and the Runes show the ways back to RÛNA.

The meaning of all this for the Initiation of the individual, for self-development is this: A quality, goal or aim can be sought as the Mystery or Hidden seed-principle in the root of any opposite quality. For example, light is the mystery of darkness, pleasure is the mystery of pain, strength is the mystery of weakness, and life is the mystery of death. In this latter regard, we only have to look at the form and result of the Wewelsburg Working carried out by Michael Aquino

---

* See, for example, discussions throughout Benjamin Walker's *Gnosticism*.

(19.10.1982ev) in the Hall of the Dead in the center of the Black Order's headquarters, the result of which was LIFE!

Becoming (*xeper*) is the Word of the worlds (Æons), the construct upon which the cycles of manifestation are actualized in the noumenological and well as phenomenological worlds. RÛNA (Gk. μυστηριον), on the other hand, is the Word of Words and of Works. It lies partially outside Becoming, and partially inside it. The genesis of consciousness was dependent upon Mystery. The Becoming of intelligence continues to be dependent upon Mystery. Without the Unknown Knowledge is impossible. If RÛNA were ever to "cease to exist" so too at that very "moment" would consciousness cease to be in the cosmos.

Glossary

This glossary of technical words sometimes employed in the talks indicates the exact definitions of words that might be used in unfamiliar contexts. The Old English (OE) or Old Norse (ON) terms from which some of these technical terms are ultimately derived are also provided.

Áss, pl. Æsir ON [pron. "au-ss"; "ayss-eer"]: The gods of consciousness in the Teutonic pantheon, governing the powers of sovereignty and physical force.
Asgard: The enclosure of the gods, the realm where the gods and goddesses exist. (ON *Ásgarðr*)
athem: The "breath of life," the vital force of life borne in the breath. (OE *æthm*; ON *önd*)
etin: A "giant," which is a living entity of great age, strength, and often knowledge. (ON *jötunn*; *jötnar*)
folk: 1) The Teutonic or Germanic nation (all people of Teutonic heritage, German, English, Dutch, Scandinavian, etc.), 2) The people gathered for a holy event.
holy: There are two aspects to this term: 1) that which is filled with divine power, and 2) that which is marked off and separate from the profane.
hugh: The cognitive part of the soul, the intellect or "mind." Also called hidge. (OE *hyge*)
hyde: The quasi-physical part of the soul which gives a person shape and form. (ON *hamr*)
lore: The tradition in all its aspects.
lyke: The physical part of the soul-body (psycho-physical) complex. Also called lich. (OE *lic*)
Midgard: the dwelling place of humanity, the physical plane of existence. Also, Mid-yard, the enclosure in the midst of all. (OE *Middangeard*; ON *Miðgarðr*)
mynd: The reflective part of the soul, the memory: personal and transpersonal. (OE *mynd*; ON *minni*)

occultnik: One who believes in things because he or she does not understand them. Devoted to the unknown for its own sake. Prone to utter such things as: "Wow, man," etc.

Reyn til Rúna: Icelandic (ON) phrase [pron. "rayn till roona" or "rain till roona"]: "Seek toward the Runes (Mysteries)." The extended formula of RÛNA.

RÛNA: The Word of Edred, often translated as "Sense of the Hidden," in its superficial understanding: Mystery, the Hidden, the Unknown. This is the sense that drives consciousness to work toward Self-Actualization.

Runer: One who undertakes to actualize the meaning of the mandate of Reyn til Rúna, one who seeks the Mystery in Life.

runestave(s): The sensible (e.g. visible and audible) manifestations of the Runes in Midgard.

soul: 1) A general term for the psychic parts of the psycho-physical complex, 2) The postmortem shade. (OE *sâwl*)

thew(s): virtue(s), or "strength(s)."

thurs(es): Natural forces of non-consciousness.

troth: Religion, being loyal to the gods and goddesses and cultural values of the ancestors. (ON *trú*, OE *treoþ*)

true: Adjectival form of "troth," can mean "loyal." A "true man" is a man loyal to the gods and goddesses of his ancestors.

Walhalla [pron. vahl-hallah]: The Hall of the Chosen (Elected), the highest enclosure of the sovereign powers of consciousness in the world order. (ON *Valhöll*.)

wode: An emotive, synthesizing part of the soul which brings various aspects together in a powerful and inspired way. Related to the mood. (OE *wôd*, ON *óðr*) world: The psycho-chronic human aspects of the manifested universe. (OE *weoruld*, the age of a man.) The cosmos, ordered world.

wyrd: The process of the unseen web of synchronicity and cause and effect throughout the cosmos. Derived from the verb meaning "to become." Same as weird.

Bibliography of Works Cited or Used as Source Material

Aquino, Michael A. *Book of Coming forth by Night: Analysis and Commentary*. San Francisco: Temple of Set, various dates.

Aureleus, Marcus. *Meditations*. tr. Maxwell Staniforth. Baltimore: Penguin, 1964.

Bachoffen, Johann Jakob. *Myth, Religion and Mother Right*. tr. R. Manheim. Princeton: Princeton University Press, 1967 [1848].

Baetke, Walter. *Das Heilige im Germanischen*. Tübingen: Mohr, 1942.

Bauschatz, Paul C. "The Germanic Ritual Feast." In: *The Nordic Languages and Modern Linguistics 3*, Ed. John M. Weinstock. Austin: University of Texas Press, 1976.

——————. *The Well and the Tree: World and Time in Early Germanic Culture*. Amherst: University of Massachusetts Press, 1982.

Benoist, Alain de. *Heide sein zu einem neuen Anfang. Die europäische Glaubensalternitive*. tr. P. d. Trevillert. (= Thule Seminar 2) Tübingen: Grabert, 1981.

Benveniste, Emile. *Indo-European Language and Society*. tr. E. Palmer. Coral Gables, FL: University of Miami Press, 1973.

Campbell, Joseph. *The Hero with a Thousand Faces*. (= Bollingen Series 17) Princeton: Princeton University Press, 1949.

Cassierer, Ernst, et al. eds. *The Renaissance Philosophy of Man*. Chicago: University of Chicago Press, 1948.

Chaney, William A. *The Cult of Kingship in Anglo-Saxon England*. Berkeley: University of California Press, 1970.

Cleasby, Richard, Guðbrand Vigfusson and William Craigie, eds. *An Icelandic-English Dictionary*. Oxford: Oxford University Press, 2nd. ed., 1957.

Cornford, Francis M, tr. and ed. *The Republic of Plato.*
Oxford: Oxford University Press, 1941.
Crowley, Aleister. *The Book of the Law.* New York: Magickal
Childe, 1990 [1938].
——————————. *Magick.* York Beach, ME: Samuel Weiser,
1973 [1929].
Davidson, Hilda R. (Ellis). *The Road to Hel.* Cambridge:
Cambridge University Press, 1943.
Davidson, H.R. Ellis. *Gods and Myths of Northern Europe.*
Harmondsworth: Penguin, 1964.
Davidson, H.R. Ellis. *Myths and Symbols in Pagan Europe.*
Syracuse, NY: Syracuse University Press, 1988.
Doresse, Jean. *The Secret Books of the Egyptian Gnostics.*
Rochester, VT: Inner Traditions, 1986.
Düwel, Klaus. *Runenkunde.* (= Sammlung Metzler 72)
Stuttgart: Metzler, 1968.
Dumézil, Georges. *Gods of the Ancient Northmen.* E. Haugen,
ed. Berkeley: University of California Press, 1973.
Eckhardt, Karl August. *Irdische Unsterblichkeit:
Germanischer Glaube an die Wiederverkörperung in der
Sippe.* Weimar: Bohlaus, 1937.
Eliade, Mircea. *Rites and Symbols of Initiation.* tr. W.
Trask. New York: Harper and Row, 1958. (Also published
as *Birth and Rebirth.*)
——————————. *The Myth of the Eternal Return or Cosmos and
History.* (=Bollingen Series 46) tr. W. Trask.
Princeton: Princeton University Press, 1971 [1954].
——————————. *A History of Religious Ideas.* tr. W. Trask.
Chicago: University of Chicago Press, 1978-1985, 3
vols.
Elliott, Ralph. *Runes: An Introduction.* Manchester:
Manchester University Press, 1959.
Fowles, John. *The Aristos.* New York: New American Library,
Second Revised Edition, 1970.
Flowers, Stephen E. "Revival of Germanic Religion in
Contemporary Anglo-American Culture." *Mankind
Quarterly,* 21:3 (1981), pp. 279-294.

———————. "Toward an Archaic Germanic Psychology." *Journal of Indo-European Studies*, 1:1-2 (193), pp. 117-138.

———————. *Runes and Magic: Magical Formulaic Elements in the Older Tradition*. New York: Lang, 1986.

———————. *The Galdrabók: An Icelandic Grimoire*. York Beach, ME: Weiser, 1988.

Flowers, S(tephen) Edred. *Fire and Ice*. St. Paul, MN: Llewellyn, 1990.

Gennep, Arnold van. *The Rites of Passage*. trs. M.B. Vizdom and G.L. Caffee. Chicago: University of Chicago Press, 1960.

Goethe, Johann Wolfgang von. *Faust: Eine Tradödie*. Erich Trunz, ed. Munich: Beck, 1976.

Grimm, Jacob. *Teutonic Mythology*. tr. S. Stallybrass. New York: Dover, 1966, 4 vols. (first published 1835).

Grønbech, Vilhelm. *The Culture of the Teutons*. London: Oxford University Press, 1931, 2 vols.

Heffner, R-M. S., et al. eds. *Goethe's Faust*. Lexington, MA: Heath, 1954.

Hieronimus, Ekkehard. *Der Traum von den Urkulturen*. (= Karl Friedrich von Siemens Stiftung. Themen XXII) Mucnich: Siemens Stiftung, 1975.

Höfler, Otto. *Kultische Geheimbünde der Germanen*. Frankfurt/Main: Diesterweg, 1934

Hollander, Lee M., tr. *The Poetic Edda*. Austin, TX: University of Texas Press, 1962.

Jacobi, Jolande. *The Psychology of C.G. Jung*. New Haven: Yale University Press, 1973 [1942].

Krause, Wolfgang. *Was man in Runen ritzte*. Halle/Saale: Niemeyer, 1935.

———————. *Runeninschriften im älteren Futhark*. (= Königsberger Gelehrten Gesellschaft 13:4) Halle/Saale: Niemeyer, 1937.

———————. *Runen*. (= Sammlung Göschen 1244/1244a) Berlin: de Gruyter, 1970.

Krebs, Pierre, ed. *Das unvergängliche Erbe: Alternativen zum Prinzip der Gleichheit.* (= Thule Seminar 1) Tübingen: Grabert, 1981.

LaVey, Anton Szandor. *The Satanic Bible.* New York: Avon, 1969.

——————————. *The Satanic Rituals.* New York: Avon, 1972.

List, Guido von. *Das Geheimnis der Runen.* (= Guido von List Bücherei 1) Vienna: Guido-von-List-Gesellschaft, 1908.

——————————. *The Secret of the Runes.* Translated by Stephen E. Flowers. Rochester, VT: Destiny Books, 1988.

Littleton, C. Scott. *The New Comparative Mythology: An Anthropological Assessment of the Theories of Georges Dumézil.* Berkeley: University of California Press, 1973, 2nd ed.

Mallory, J. P. *In Search of the Indo-Europeans: Language, Archaeology and Myth.* London: Thames & Hudson, 1989.

Miller, David L. *The New Polytheism: Rebirth of the Gods and Goddesses.* New York: Harper and Row, 1974.

Neckel, Gustav and hans Kuhn. *Edda: Die Lieder des Codex Regius nebst verwandten Denkmälern.* Heidelberg: Winter, 1962.

Nietzsche, Friedrich. *The Birth of Tragedy.* tr. W. Kaufman. New York: Vintage, 1967 [1972].

Olsen, Magnus. "Om Trollruner." *Edda* 5 (1916), 225-45.

Orwell, George. "Politics and the English Language." In: *The George Orwell Reader.* ed. Richard H. Revere. New York: Harcourt Brace and Javonovitch, 1984.

Otto, Rudolf. *The Idea of the Holy.* tr. J.W. Harvey. Oxford: Oxford University Press, 1958.

Polomé, Edgar C. "Some Comments of Voluspa Stanzas 17-18." In: Polomé, E.C. ed. Old Norse Literature and Mythology: A Symposium. Austin, TX: University of Texas Press, 1969, pp. 265-290.

———————. "The Indo-European Component in Germanic Religion." In: *Myth and Law among the Indo-Europeans: Studies in Comparative Indo-European Mythology*. ed. J. Puhvel. Berkeley: University of California Press, 1970.
———————. "Approaches to Germanic Mythology." In: *Myth in Indo-European Antiquity*. Berkeley: Univestity of California Press, 1974.
Scholem, Gershom. *Kabbalah*. New York: New American Library, 1978.
Schröder, Franz Rolf. *Altgermanische Kulturprobleme*. (= Trübners Philologische Bibliothek 11) Berlin: de Gruyter, 1929.
Seznec, Jean. *The Survival of the Pagan Gods*. tr. B. Sessions. New York: Harper and Row, 1953.
Spiesberger, Karl. *Runen Magie*. Berlin: Schikowski, 1955.
Sturluson, Snorri. *Edda*. Ed. Anne Holtsmark and Jon Helgason. Copenhagen: Munksgaard, 1976.
———————. *The Prose Edda*. Tr. A. Brodeur. New York: American Scandinavian Foundation, 1929.
Tacitus, Cornelius. *The Agricola and the Germania*. tr. H. Mattingly. Harmondsworth: Penguin, 1948.
Thorsson, Edred. *Futhark: A Handbook of Rune Magic*. York Beach, ME: Weiser, 1984.
———————. *Runelore: A Handbook of Esoteric Runology*. York Beach, ME: Weiser, 1987.
———————. *At the Well of Wyrd: A Handbook of Runic Divination*. York Beach, ME: Weiser, 1988
———————. *Rune Might: Secret Practices of the German Rune Magicians*. St. Paul, MN: Llewellyn, 1989.
———————. *A Book of Troth*. St. Paul, MN: Llewellyn, 1989.
Turville-Petre, E.O.G. *Myth and Religion of the North*. New York: Holt, Rinehart and Winston, 1964.
Vries, Jan de. *Altgermanische Religionsgeschichte*. Berlin: de Gruyter, 1956-57, 2 vols.
———————. *Altnordisches etymologisches Wörterbuch*. Leiden: Brill, 1961.

Walker, Benjamin. *Gnosticism: Its History and Influence.* Wellingborough, UK: Aquarian Press, 1983.

Warrack, Alexander. *Scots Dialect Dictionary.* Edinburgh: Lomond, 1911.

Waterfield, Robin, tr. *Theology of Arithmetic.* Grand Rapids, MI: Phanes, 1988.

Zoller, Robert. *Skaldic Number-Lore.* Austin: The Rune-Gild. 1986.

——————. *Towards a Germanic Esoteric Astronomy.* Austin: The Rune-Gild, 1986.

www.ingramcontent.com/pod-product-compliance
Lightning Source LLC
Chambersburg PA
CBHW031213090426
42736CB00009B/899